Bob + Jenny,

from all of us at

Mc Kingsmith

Jill Oct 2002

Images of Peeblesshire

by

Liz Hanson

LIZ HANSON IMAGES
82 Dalatho Crescent
Peebles EH45 8DU

First published in 1993 by
LIZ HANSON IMAGES
82 Dalatho Crescent
Peebles EH45 8DU

ISBN 1 898381 00 3

Printed by Buccleuch Printers Ltd., Carnarvon Street, Hawick TD9 7EB

All photographs by Liz Hanson

THE PUBLISHER WISHES TO ACKNOWLEDGE THE ENCOURAGEMENT OF TWEEDDALE DISTRICT COUNCIL
AND FINANCIAL ASSISTANCE IN THE PRODUCTION OF THIS BOOK

Front Cover: View from Cademuir Hill

This book is dedicated to my late father,
John Hanson

River Tweed at Cardrona

Foreword

I remember vividly my first impression of Peeblesshire. It was 1970, and I was taking the route south from Edinburgh. As the panorama opened up on the descent from Leadburn, I was struck by the backdrop of splendid hills in the distance. With the passage of time, I have come to know these hills intimately, as I have been privileged to live in this unspoilt area of Scotland for 15 years.

Apart from its northern boundaries, the landscape is dominated by hills, and the valleys of the River Tweed and its tributaries. During the years of exploration of this countryside, I have never ceased to be astonished and delighted by the spectrum of colour to be found at all times of the year; I have tried to reflect this in the collection of photographs making up this book.

Peeblesshire is an area endowed with a wealth of natural beauty, and much may be overlooked if visitors limit their journey to the County town of Peebles, delightful though it is. In compiling this book, my intention has been to share some glimpses of this beauty with others and perhaps inspire them to seek it out further for themselves. The format is broadly seasonal, and I have focused on the intrinsic qualities of the countryside, rather than traditional tourist locations, adequately catered for in other publications. The geographical coverage does not claim to be comprehensive, and I am conscious of some notable omissions: this is due entirely to restrictions of space, which in turn is dictated by considerations of a financial nature! To those communities or areas not included, I apologise; to those appearing in the book, I extend my thanks for the inspiration they provided, and hope my representation is to their liking.

CARLOPS

WEST
LINTON

Lyne Water

A701

A703

ROMANNO
BRIDGE

BLYTH
BRIDGE

Eddleston Water

EDDLESTON

A702

PEEBLES

Leithen Water

A72

SKIRLING

BROUGHTON

Manor Water

INNERLEITHEN

WALKERBURN

TRAQUAIR

Holms Water

River Tweed

TWEEDSMUIR

A701

PEEBLESSHIRE

Map supplied by Tweeddale District Council
Not drawn to scale

Looking west from ridge above Kilbucho, Broughton

January morning mist over Kirkton Manor

Hundleshope Heights from Hamilton Hill

Ploughing, Easter Happrew

Sheildgreen Kips from Jedderfield

Spring flowers

Above: Spring Snowflake, Kailzie Gardens
Right: Snowdrops, Traquair

Above: Winter Aconites, Kailzie Gardens
Right: Wild Daffodils, Dawyck Botanic Gardens

Above: Red Squirrel, Cardrona
Right: Pair of Goosander, Cuddyside

Grey Heron, March Street Weir, Peebles

Drystane dyke and sheep, Tweedsmuir. Culter Fell is in the distance.

West Linton from Castlelaw

Stanhope and the Tweedsmuir Hills

View of Barns House and Haswellsykes

Bogsbank

Sheep and partridges, Southpark, Peebles

Sheep at Drochil

Spring day, Peebles

Lambs, Lyne

Duck silhouettes

Pair of Mallard ducks

Pair of Mallard ducklings

Rachan Pool

River Tweed, Dawyck

Left: Upper Cuddyside
Above: Dawyck Mill Bridge

Wall-loving plants include Fairy Foxglove (above) and Ivy Leaved Toadflax adorning the post box at Stobo (far right).
Right: Also at Stobo, new and old telephone boxes – the latter has unfortunately been removed.

Hundleshope Heights

Rosebay Willow Herb, Neidpath Castle

Wild flower display (Pink Campion and Green Alkanet), Glensax

Man-made arrangement, Hay Lodge

Reflections, Dawyck Mill

Alder reflections, Hallmanor

Evening sunlight, Broughton Place

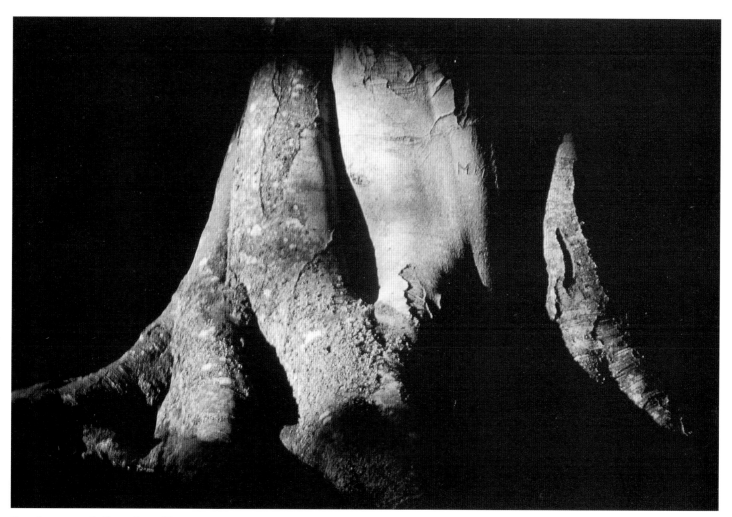

Beech tree trunk, Broughton Place

Scots Pines, Dreva

Left: Long evening shadows, Drumelzier
Above: Autumn, Drumelzier Glen

Far left: Jigsaw field, near Eddleston. Above left: Fallen leaves. Below left: Lime trees, Kingsmeadows House.
Above: Kailzie and Lee Pen

Autumn light, Peebles

Peebles and The Hydro in Autumn

Dawyck, near Crownhead Bridge

Above: Red-berried Elder
Right: Rowan berries with Bullfinch

Looking across Drumelzier Glen to Finglen Rig

Snow clouds approaching Eddleston

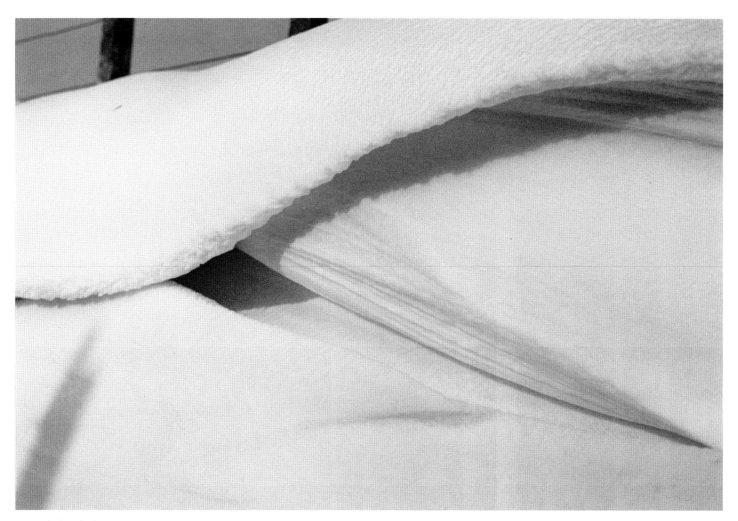

Snowdrift, Skirling

Ice on River Tweed

Left: Snow shower over Broad Law. Above: Low cloud, Crookston.

Before . . .   *After . . .*   *During . . .*

Winter feeding at Traquair

Above: Hay Heck
Right: Turnip field

Winter's day, Peebles